Get

Your

Balls

Back

For Happy Relationships

Brigitte Sumner

My Voice Publishing
Unit 1 16 Maple Road
EASTBOURNE
BN23 6NY

United Kingdom

www.myvoicepublishing.com

Published by MVP July 2010

© Brigitte Sumner 2010

Brigitte Sumner asserts the moral right to be identified as the author of this work

Cover design: Southeast DM Ltd

Design: Southeast DM Ltd

ISBN 978-0-9554692-7-5

Contents

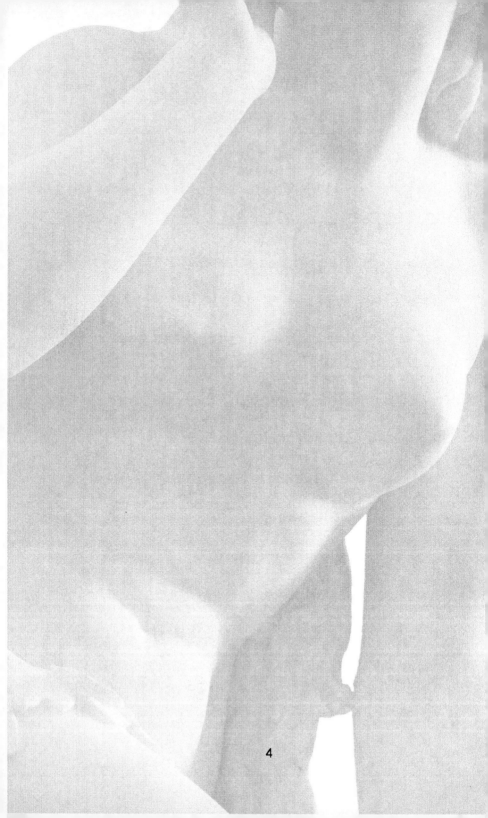

4

Introduction

There were a few seconds of silence. The eager and young man said *'go and do your chores in the house.'* The rest of the audience stayed very still. At the other side of the room people started to shuffle and one or two nervous giggles were heard. People were uncomfortable with the statement. The young man was the youngest in the audience.

I was running a workshop about feminine and masculine energies. We spoke about how the authentic masculine would address the authentic feminine.

The exercise was to translate harsh language spoken between men and women in relationship into what you really meant. To improve communication. To ensure love stayed. The sentence he wanted to translate was *'you're always watching television.'* The young man in question was about nineteen and quite eager. He really wanted to get it right. She was watching television too long and what he really meant to say was *'I want to spend some time with you.'*

Somehow the reaction of the audience told me that no one thought this was a great idea. I asked around what people thought. *'Terrible.'* *'Makes it worse.'* *'I'd file for divorce,'* a middle aged lady at the back of the room shouted. The young man was slightly less certain and eager. *'Ok guys, help him out,'* I encouraged, feeling a bit sorry for this apprentice. *'How about let's clean our bedroom together, I vacuum and you dust, race you, and after we watch a movie together?'* a man, about mid-thirties in the middle of the room volunteered. A sigh of relief. People started to breathe again. The young man smiled but seemed a bit puzzled.

This was an example of how uneducated we really are in the area of relationships. It is not a subject at school. We largely don't learn this from our elders. I don't know about you but from the age of twelve I had to rush downstairs after doing my homework to referee their conversations. My parents' relationship was filled with the joy of the three of us as well as financial disasters, emotional minefields, cultural differences, absent extended family support as well as post war economic stress that many of my generation share.

Communication between people has always fascinated me. I continuously look for ways to simplify things and build bridges. You often teach what you yourself are bad at, so I must confess that I am the worst communicator at times. I am learning. I am a slow learner. I know it will take me the rest of this lifetime and probably more to come to improve.

I have always enjoyed observing people. From a young age, I watched and listened. That came in handy when it became my career and profession. My career path went from teacher to communication trainer to coach to speaker and writer. My passion is to share ways that I have found to make life happier.

This book is written on request. When I wrote Give Him Back His Balls, men asked *'when is Get Your Balls Back'* coming out? I said *'never'* as I felt that I could not write that book. I am not a man. For years that was the standard answer. Until someone (a man!) suggested I interview men. This book is a result of years of interviews, interactions, sessions, workshops and observations from everyday life.

I do not vow to be an expert in this field. I come from compassion. I am mother to two boys, who I have watched while growing up. They are men now. Their little friends who were small boys once, now also are grown men. All grown men have been like those small boys once. Full of expectation of life. Of love.

I believe we all deserve passionate and loving intimate relationships. I believe this is everyone's birthright. I believe there is not enough education and information on how to create and sustain a loving relationship. That must be why there are a lot of books about relationships. This book may give you another perspective, another small tool or maybe just the realisation that you're not the only one.

I wish for you a life where you feel comfortable with whom you are.

I wish for you happy and fulfilling relationships.

Brigitte Sumner.

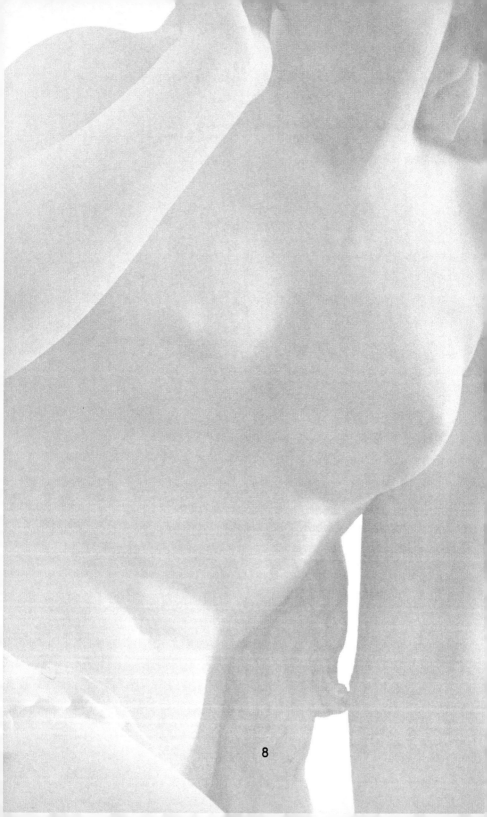

8

When a man's in his 20's, he plays football

...In his 30's, he plays cricket

...In his 40's, he plays snooker

...In his 50's he plays golf

... Obviously as you get older...

...your balls get smaller

Little baby boys

Growing up to be big men

Promising the world

Chapter One:

Growing Up

We are conditioned by culture, upbringing and education. In order to function in a safe and working environment we have to behave and conform to certain standards. From the day we are born we get 'trained' into certain behaviour.

We have our primary needs met by our parents. In the ideal world, we were all wanted, loved and adored for just being a white/pink/yellow/brown/black little helpless bundle that would sleep, feed, urinate and defecate at times. The only thing we would need to do in turn is exist and just for that we would receive unconditional love.

Depending on which expert was in vogue at the time when we were little, we were either left to our own devices when crying ('they seek attention; you create spoiled children and a rod for your own back'). Or picked up when crying ('they are conveying a need and have no other way of telling their parents'). Or never had to go so far as crying ('you can tell what your baby needs by being so connected to him/her that you can anticipate what he/she needs'). All these different approaches have different effects on how we turn out as children and eventually as adults.

Early on, we were praised for smiling and gurgling. We were encouraged to burp and our bowel movements were topics of regular and open conversation. Farts were a source of amusement and those around us said 'better out than in' in a matter of fact way. This was generally a happy time. We knew the boundaries.

We found out rapidly how to make those that we depended on, happy.

Then all changed. Nobody told us. The goalposts moved. Almost overnight! What we did in our pants, all of a sudden had to be done in a bowl. If we were lucky, the bowl was more or less child size. If we were not, the bowl came at least up to our eyebrows and made a horrendous noise and subsequently swallowed all that it could gulp in its huge opening of a mouth. Very scary stuff!

Instead of letting all go, we had to hang on. That could become uncomfortable. Sit on this huge bowl. Fight our fears of being swallowed whole by this enormous monster. And relax and finally let go. Very confusing indeed.

Burping got out of fashion. Another rule that was invented overnight and no one told us about. Burping you just don't do. Certainly not in public. We might try it again every once in a while to see whether it has come back in fashion? Being told off. I guess it has not come back in fashion.....

And of course we never even noticed that we farted. It just sort of happened all by itself. At around the same time that burping becomes illegal farting is even more of a no-no.

You can see that this is the most confusing time for a child growing up. From the little creature that can do no wrong, we become persons who have to account for their own actions. Our parents do the best with the resources they have. Even if we feel that our childhood has been terrible, we can find ways to step into their shoes and forgive.

Our parents' behaviour has an impact on ours. We all have our 'bagage'. We react from our conditioning. What has happened during your childhood has shaped you. Those patterns are still ingrained and invoke reactions now.

Raising our two sons has been one of the most rewarding times of my life. I still regard the opportunity to watch and observe them develop and grow up to be one of the best gifts. I strongly believe that children come through you, but you do not own them.

Being a modern mother who spent a good part of her life in a woman's' Lib capital (Amsterdam), I had no inclination to raise my children to be either more masculine or more feminine. I did not want to push them in either direction. For both Rex and I, it was important that they grew up to be confident, happy and healthy citizens with the ability to think for themselves.

In our sons' toy box were stuffed animals, dolls, building bricks, cars and prams. They were able to build dens or look after their dolls and animals if they wished to do so which they did at times. The garden and home provided for exploring, being in nature and creativity. There was a huge dressing up case with anything from pirates clothes to princess clothes. There were dresses, trousers, hats for both genders, wigs with blonde hair, curly red and black punk rock. There were clogs (I am Dutch), boots and stiletto heels.

The youngest had a fancy for purple and anything bling. He would frequently be running around with a red, short wig, a liftboy top and a purple curtain to complete the outfit. His other favourite was a batman mask that I had fashioned from a T-shirt that was too small, with a pirate top. The eldest took a fancy to a Billy Jack hat that was miles too big for him. With that he rode around on a stick horse made from one of Rex's old socks. At times he added a pair of high heeled boots to this. This outfit seemed to call for a deep and drawn out voice and serious face. When they were too hot, they wore no clothes and played with the hosepipe, buckets and paddling pools.

Although Rex had been in the army as a young man, he was ambivalent to my wish not to encourage violence in the shape of guns and other weaponry.

As soon as they went to play at friends, they saw all kinds of wonderful guns, pistols and such. Because they did not have anything like that at home, it turned out to become the one thing they wanted most. Soon they created guns from Lego, sticks, brooms and even a Barbie doll with legs wide apart would double up as a very inventive and noisy shooting implement.

As I noticed that my intentions had the opposite effect, I went out to buy as many guns as I could at a car boot sale one Sunday morning. They played with the dozens of guns for about a week after which the newness wore off and they abandoned them, after which their play became less gun centred.

The dolls were rarely played with. At times they were plonked into the prams and raced around the drive. My comments along the lines of 'o, poor dolly, she must get very carsick' were ignored or met with funny looks.

Up until the age of ten, there was not a huge difference in how they related to their boy friends or girl friends. After ten, these differences became more apparent.

The girls would talk more, the boys would talk less. The boys played more physical games when they got together and would have the odd tomboy joining in.

Obvious differences in dexterity and development between the boys and girls between the ages of ten to thirteen seemed to lead to a lot of competition amongst and between the genders. Parents nurtured latent, obvious, and sometimes even absent talent and ferried children far and wide in order to encourage new found strengths and hobbies.

Children in their early teens were spotted as Wimbledon potentials, sponsored to train with well known football clubs or had extra curricular lessons in singing, violin and piano. You never knew whether you were taking them to gymnastics, collecting them from piano lessons or supporting a swim gala.

Body parts starting to grow. Arms extended. Legs looked like stilts. Never ending. The notches moving up on the doorjamb, witnessed what we as parents did not see on a day to day basis. My youngest showed me every new hair that sprouted from his armpits (until there were about ten). We studied hair on his upper lip together. If you looked really hard in broad daylight he had what he proudly called a 'moustache' by the age of thirteen. As he inherited more of the Caucasian genes than his brother, he is more hairy and lighter skinned. At times, I still get invited to gaze into those more and more hairy places, which I choose to consider being a privilege.

The age of being puzzled by the other gender started slowly. Hormones kicked in, voices lowered. Girls giggled, were silly. Didn't play ball, but were intriguing. The girls congregated together, whispered and threw glances at the boys. There was the initial focus on their sports, their academics. Their new found agility, loss of clumsiness and height of physical strength and power, a thrill to explore. Later the notion came that the whispering was actually about them. The boys were so preoccupied with all this change that it took them a while to find that they were attractive to the girls.

In the same way, the girls became more and more attractive to them. Girls, who until not long ago were their equals in maths, their pals in gymnastics and games of hide and seek. Unnoticed they had grown into young women. With breasts, hips and luscious hair, where previously were bony contours and a functional ponytail. They had grown into their once too large teeth. Had seductive smiles. And pretty eyes.

Mixed parties. Messing about with adult drinks and other pastimes.

Wanting to be treated like a grown up. Rebelling against parents. Driving lessons. School exams. Opportunities. Being treated like an adult when breaking the law. Sobering experiences. Realising that all choices bear consequences.

Confused boys in our living room around the age of fifteen, sixteen. Gathered around a mobile phone, reading a text. Why does she write that??? Does that mean she likes me or she doesn't??? What should I write back? No idea what she means. Texting something funny back, that would have worked with a mate. 'Hi, I like u coz you ave big boobs.' Goes down like a lead balloon. All communication stops....

Ask a girl. Can you translate? How about writing 'I like you, do you want to go out with me?' Rapid response 'I like you too, yes, let's go out.' The boys are puzzled; they thought the first communication was much more complementary. They go out, a date it is. Now where? Snogging? O, dear, too soon. End of date. Next.

When do you start to snog then? Well, not during the first five minutes. You talk, the way you'd talk to your sister. Or your Mum, or maybe even your Gran. 'Your hair looks nice. Did you watch this movie? Have you read that book? You are really clever. Can I buy you a drink? Do you want to go for a walk?' At this age, boys can be very shy. In order to have any chance with the girls, you must get good at making conversation (at any age). Mums can help. By addressing the 'matey' language and teach them that this is not the way to talk to a girl/woman.

The Social Organisation of Sexuality: Sexual Practices in the United States found that 54 per cent of men reported thinking about sex every day or several times a day. At the same time there is pressure from society to perform well (at school) and to conform (to society's rules). They have an urge to experiment, with life.

At this stage, the parents who proclaimed that they could very well have spawned the next David Beckham, Charlotte Church or Michael Jordan quietly disappear from the scene.

The next time you meet their son, his eyes turn around clockwise at the speed of light and the pupils are so dilated that you cannot discern their colour.

Four years on, the Charlotte Church wannabe, sports hair in five different colours and stumbles along on the arm of a chap with matching hairdo and piercings.

When you have managed to tip toe around the mine field that is communication with the other gender during your young man years, you can progress and consider a relationship. Going out with someone consistently and not having sex with anyone else is considered to be a relationship. Sounds like a heavy word.

Now you are together with her. Now what? On your mind is sex, every four minutes. On her mind is romance and possibly sex at the end of more romance. What is romance? Romance is holding hands, standing together, doing things together, and having a meal together. Going to see a movie, a show, having a drink together. Sitting and watching television together can be romance too. Going for a walk together. The young man naturally will want to rush or even skip this part.

Exercise:

-How did you grow up?

-Is there anything from your childhood that needs to be cleared up?

-Do you need to let go of any behaviour that does not work for you at the age you are now that stems from your younger years?

-Do you need to let go of any stories that stop you from growing up?

Are you true to you?

Do you live your life as you?

Or somebody else?

Chapter Two:

Do you have balls?

How do you know whether you have balls or not? You can do this quiz to find out.

Q   U   I   Z

1. You are sitting in the pub with a group of male friends. A pretty girl walks by. What do you do?

a) You make loud, lewd comments and whistle after her.

b) You haven't even noticed her.

c) When your friends comment on her, you nod and move the conversation on to something else.

d) You have a good look and appreciate what you see without feeling the need to make a lewd comment.

2. You and your date are going to the movies. What happens?

a) You have picked your choice of movie and happily share your drink and popcorn with her when she asks.

b) You expect her to pick a movie and collect you from work.

c) You have chosen the movie together and she picks up the tickets whilst you buy the popcorn.

d) You have chosen a movie that you think she'll enjoy and have bought the tickets beforehand.

3. You and your date are driving along a route that you are both unfamiliar with on your way to a party. What happens?

a) You boast that you know the way everywhere, turn off the navigation system and arrive two hours late in a bad mood.

b) You read the paper whilst she gets you there.

c) You both look at the map, have an argument and get hopelessly lost for hours.

d) Even though you are lost, you know how to read a map. You pull over, find out on the map where to go and drive there, getting you to the party more or less on time.

4. You and your partner are having an argument. Which is the most likely scenario?

a) You shout at her and may even hit her.

b) You don't like arguments so you stay still and ignore her.

c) You are both throwing daggers with words. First you each storm off in a huff, then you talk a few hours later.

d) You recognize that she needs to let these feelings out. You know this is not about you, so you listen and she calms down. The storm blows over soon.

5. What are you most likely to be overheard saying?

a) Women are weaker than men.

b) Men are weaker than women.

c) Women and men are the same in every way.

d) Women and men complement each other. We all have masculine and feminine energies that surface at different times.

6. You go on holiday with your wife. What do you pack?

a) My sports gear as I will spend all my days on the golf course/ hunting/on the tennis court etc.

b) Whatever she tells me to.

c) We pack together and have lengthy discussions about each item.

d) A few changes of underwear, a book, enough clean shirts, something nice for when we go out and a fishing rod.

7. The kids are having an argument. It looks as if one of them is going to get hurt. What do you do?

a) You shout and thump both of them.

b) You ask your wife to sort them out.

c) You tell them that it is not nice to argue and that they should play quietly.

d) You keep an eye on them, knowing that their squabbles can make them stronger. If needed you intervene or distract them and give each child a task to do to keep them occupied together.

8. You have to work late in the office. What do you do?

a) You don't phone, your wife will get the message when you don't show for dinner.

b) You phone your wife and grovel for her permission to stay late.

c) You ask your secretary to phone your wife to tell her.

d) You phone your wife, explain the situation and tell her you love her.

9. You want to make love to your partner. You are in bed, what do you do?

a) Tell her to get her kit off.

b) Whine about her wearing a nightdress without making any advances.

c) You ask her politely if she's in the mood.

d) You give her a foot massage, then with a mischievous grin rip off her nightie with your teeth and get down to it!

10 Your idea of the future for your family is:

a) For me to have a bigger car.

b) No idea, she's in charge and I'm sure she'll let me know in due course.

c) We have discussed this together in depth, but there is scope for change.

d) We know where we're going. My partner knows that I'll do everything in my power to ensure we keep on track whilst checking in regularly to ensure that both our needs are still being met.

11. Your mother has moved in with you. What happens?

a) I am sure the women sort the housework out between them.

b) Mother gets all the attention she wants from me which is more than my partner gets.

c) I make sure I divide my attention equally between my mother and my partner.

d) I make my mother welcome and let her know that my partner is number one in my life.

MOSTLY A: You live from an energy that you believe to be masculine but isn't really. This type of behaviour is violent and unnecessary. This energy tends to create challenges in relationships.

MOSTLY B: You do not live in your masculine energy most of the time. Very feminine women may not be attracted to you. You attract women who want to mother you, or control you in some other way. If you want to change that, make sure to live more from your masculine energy.

MOSTLY C: At times you live in your masculine energy and at times in your feminine energy. You may not be perceived as a very masculine man and will probably attract a partner who lives less in her feminine energy. If you want to change this, then display more of your masculine energy.

MOSTLY D: You live in your masculine energy most of the time. You will mostly attract women who are mostly in their feminine energy. Men who are not masculine may be daunted by you at times. (please note: for same gender relationships, the words man and woman can be interchanged)

We all see and live examples of inauthentic and authentic masculinity on a daily basis. Both these terms are just a description and not an absolute truth. Men and women have masculine AND feminine energies. In order to fully develop and grow, we all need to embrace both of those energies. In Eastern philosophies and practices such as T'ai Chi, Acupuncture, Chinese Medicine, Feng Shui and Qi Gong the importance of balance between the Yin and Yang, the feminine and masculine has long been recognised. One cannot exist without the other.

'Yang has its root in Yin
Yin has its root in Yang.
Without Yin, Yang cannot arise.
Without Yang, Yin cannot be born.
Yin alone cannot arise; Yang alone cannot grow.
Yin and Yang are divisible but inseparable.'
Nei Jing

In our physical bodies we are both Yin and Yang. There is a constant flow which we know as health. If this flow is disturbed we experience dis-ease. Nothing is ever entirely yin or yang. They are in balance, but this balance is fluid and changing constantly. The Yin-Yang symbol with the little white circle in the black and the little black circle in the white, shows that nothing is ever totally Yin or Yang. The symbol also shows the interdependence of the Yin and Yang and indicates that all of creation is composed of two energies held in harmony and interaction.

The Yin energy, the authentic feminine is described as dark, moist, diffuse, vague, intuitive, and receptive, i.e. 'being' energy. Within this system, men are considered predominately yang but contain a yin component and women are considered predominately yin whilst containing an element of yang. In later life, each one of us is encouraged to integrate the opposite energy in a move towards wholeness.

Inauthentic masculine energy manifests in aggressive, superior, controlling, dominant, forceful and overly competitive behaviour in relationship with the feminine.

Authentic masculine energy is often manifested in 'doing', analytical thinking, preference for concrete concepts and left brain activities, impatient, striving, thrusting, good at organizing, logical, busy and firm.

Authentic masculine energy manifests in focused, powerful, protective, helpful, supportive and loyal behaviour, being in service in relationship with the feminine.

'If any human being is to reach full maturity, both the masculine and feminine sides of the personality must be brought up into consciousness.' M. Esther Harding.

26

Geoff's Story

I spoke to Geoff. He was a farmer in the North West. His farm had been built up by his father, his grandfather and his great grandfather. From a young age, Geoff was always the one who would take over the farm. His heart was in it and he felt at home at the family farm. A young and likeable boy, Geoff was average at school, excelled at sports and could always be found outdoors on a tractor or under it mending it. He was certainly not afraid to get his hands dirty or work hard and long hours.

Having had a short fuse as a young man, Geoff had calmed down considerably. His recent divorce was as many separations: an emotional business for both and all parties involved. His appreciation for the life on the farm, observing his cattle, created a unique view on differences between men and women.

When they get into season, heifers walk through fences. The otherwise shy, calm and submissive female walks through fences and through rivers. This is the sex drive. They become unreasonable. It's the same with people. I have 18-year old twins, a boy and a girl. At times, my daughter talks about her friends in a derogatory way. All girls do. And between them, the boys and the girls, they can't communicate at all. Despite this huge pull to reproduce, they find it hard to have a conversation together.

The communication between boys and girls becomes so totally different during their teens.

Geoff never really lost his balls but can see many men who do in a similar situation. In a relationship there is a mix of needs of both people, it can become complicated. Asked by his wife, who he loved the most: her, the farm or the Labrador? The fact that he had to think about that did not please her at all. Of course at that young, Geoff had no real education of how to best deal with that question and thought 'If I can have all those three I am a better person

27

for it, I feel complete and fulfilled.' He had the vision of growing the family business. He was completely focussed. He adored his work and did not mind to get up at five or six o'clock in the morning.

He was so focussed. He can see now that he neglected other parts of life, a young wife with twin babies, toddlers later, children after a few years. He thought it would be good, but if he is honest, it wasn't. His motto was that he was doing this for the family, for his wife and to become respected.

Geoff's' advice to other men is to be careful about what you have to do and love to do. Don't ignore your partner.

Geoff wanted to work hard for some twenty years so that he could be financially free to do whatever he wanted with his wife by that time. The plan has panned out differently. Because of the divorce the cattle had to go. Now the land has been turned into arable land, which takes a third of the time, so that he can do anything he likes. Ironically. The twins are largely grown up. He has the time now they never had earlier in his marriage.

Geoff says he felt as if he lost balls once. He felt devastated. It was obvious that his wife would leave. She asked for a lot of money. He showed his upset and cried. She reacted. He knew then, that any respect she had had for him was over.

He now knows that however painful that was, it made him much stronger.

What did Geoff learn from this? Because he was on new ground during the divorce, he had to learn to find what he believed in within himself. He used to be impulsive. These days he thinks, waits a few days, until something from inside tells him what the right action is. Nowadays he trusts impeccably what that is.

There were other lows. Moments of phenomenal humility,

no real devastation but so many aspects of pride and self respect got really hammered. Geoff found that the only way through was with humility. This gave him strength.

His advice for anyone going through something tough and painful as divorce: Look back to when things were good: 'She was my best friend in the world. On her 40th Birthday, I felt this burning love for her. I was amazed; we'd been together since teens. I did not know I could still feel this. We had a big party and I hid behind some huge speakers and jumped out from behind them and gave her an enormous bouquet of roses.'

'So know I know exactly how I CAN feel, that is a benchmark and I'm not going to settle for anything less than that.'

Geoff has moved on and is Internet dating. He has met more women in three months than in his entire life. All sorts. He takes it with humour. Was nervous to start with. His last courting time was about thirty years ago. He was not comfortable with it then, and he was not good at it.

But the scene has changed. You can read about what you see in the comfort of your own armchair on dating sites. You learn techniques of how to get people interested in you. The Q and A can be exciting. You can fall in love with someone you have never met. And in many cases never will.

His advice is to be open and honest when online dating. He wants someone who is interested in him to know about his divorce, his children, his situation. Geoff is quite clear about his reason for internet dating. He wants to meet someone to spend the rest of his life with. But if he goes out with a nice lady and it stops at only lunch that is great too.

He is not in a hurry. He remembers back to his schooldays. He sat in the first row, third from the left. Divinity lesson number one. The Reverend asked a question that made all the thirteen year old boys blush, but sit up with their undivided attention *'Does sexual intercourse create a relationship or confirm one?'* A potent lesson to learn. It is now forty years on. Geoff says *'you can't 'unsleep' with someone.'*

The last bit of advice from Geoff: *'If people put only half the effort into making their relationship work as they put into their divorce more relationships would survive.'*

Exercise:

-Where do you display inauthentic masculine behaviour?

-Sum up how this is holding you back from growing in your relationship with the feminine and relationships in general.

Life throws curved balls too

Can you deal with them or not?

That's the way life is

Chapter 3:

Do you need balls?

Different cultures and situations require different levels of 'having balls.'

It will be different for you what 'having balls' means depending on the culture and society that you have grown up in and live in. Where you grew up, what pressure, demands and expectations have been placed on you from an early boyhood all play their role.

You probably had different circumstances when growing up on a cattle farm in the Midwest of the US or in the centre of Beijing, being the son of a cadre official in the government.

Or being the son of a hairdresser in Amsterdam, or the son of a bouncer in a club in Mexico City.

To generalise and to expect the same or even similar characteristics when growing up is unrealistic. There is no uniform picture of what a 'man-with-balls' should look like. When I chose the title for this book (which, lets' face it, is a title that jumps out), I did not simply want to shock your granny or your prim and proper neighbour. Honestly.

What I see as a man with balls is a man who lives his life on his terms. Following his mission, developing his vision. Yet at the same time being mindful of people, other life and the environment around him. Respectful of the planet. A man who lives life as his authentic self. A man who doesn't need to hide his authentic self for others. A man who is comfortable with whom he is.

That doesn't mean that he would never get angry. Or stressed. Or upset. Or sad. You can be all of that. At times. Be aware of your feelings. Express them when needed. In a safe environment. Without hurting others or yourself. And then move on. Get on.

With your life. Your purpose. Whatever that is for you. If you need help in doing so, seek help. There is nothing heroic about denying yourself to reach out when needed.

The man in Tokyo will live this in a different way than the man in London, who in turn will interpret this differently than the man in Bogota or Tasmania. The fisherman in Sumatra has different ways than the King of Sweden. The dustman in Berlin makes different choices than the CEO in New York City. They all have the gift and opportunity to live a life that feels authentic to them as a male human being.

How that is for you, you decide.

Women can have balls as well and the way both men and women behave complement one another. That means that at times the man is in need of a woman with balls, and the woman is in need of a man with balls. Between these, there is polarity. Where there is feminine, there is attraction to masculine. Yin complements yang. There is no high without low. No dark without light. We are all that.

Both masculine and feminine energies have power. And both are readily available to us all. That doesn't mean that it comes natural to you. You may need to work on developing your natural masculine energy. Everything around us is made up of energy. You can't always see energies. But you can feel them, sense them. And if you can't yet, you can learn how to.

Some situations require more balls. Some situations require fewer balls.

Dan's Story

Dan was hurt so many times. He really did not want to approach the woman he met during his new training course. He told me that he had not finished the financial terms with his ex-wife and that his daughters might react

34

adversely to him having a new partner.

He had not even spoken to her yet We went back to basics with just a few questions. I asked Dan if just speaking to this lady would upset his daughters? Would just having a conversation with her have any effect on his financial terms with his ex-wife? The answer to both questions was of course 'no'.

He admitted that he had talked to another woman besides his wife for fifteen years, so he was really quite nervous.

He explored if he could talk to her in the same way that he would talk to anyone who he liked, male or female alike. He did not even know if he would actually like her. He did not know whether she would like him. I asked how many ladies there were on the course. Five he said.

I asked him if it were possible that any of those five ladies fancied HIM. He was surprised, that had not occurred to him! He giggled and got where we were going with this. Yes, it was possible.

Dan relaxed. I asked the question: 'what is the worst thing that can happen when you talk to her?' 'That she doesn't want to talk to me' he said. Ok, 'what do you make that to mean?' He had to think about that one for a little. 'That there is something wrong with me', my question to that was 'that is ONE meaning, what else could it mean?' 'She is in a relationship, or she is shy, or she is in a hurry.'

We explored a little more. I asked if she could really not talk to him if she were in a relationship. He found that a little far fetched on further thought. We went on 'imagine that you talk to her, she talks to you, you meet her again over the next few sessions, you ask her out, she says 'no'. What would that mean to you?' 'That she doesn't' like me.' 'And what does that mean?' 'That I'm a loser. That I'm rejected and I hate rejection.'

'What else could it mean?' 'It could mean that she is in

35

a relationship, in which case I would respect her for not going out with me' 'it could meant that she is too busy or otherwise occupied, or that she doesn't like me.' 'Let's explore the not liking you....do YOU like everyone?' I asked. 'No, of course I don't.' 'So it is possible that not everyone likes you too, is that ok?' 'Sure.' He got the picture. The very worst thing was that she might not like him, which was ok.

As it turned out and evolved, Dan spoke to her during the subsequent training sessions. She was a pleasant and fun conversationalist and they got on very well. It was another couple of weeks before Dan plucked up the courage to ask her out. She declined. Not because she did not like him but because there were a lot of sad and intense things going on in her immediate family. Dan was fine with this. He asked her to let him know if there was anything he could do to support her. They are still friends.

We also addressed the issue with his daughters. They were ten and thirteen at the time. Women in the making. We so often forget that our sons grow into men with male behaviour and that our daughters grow into women with female behaviour. They need to respond to peer pressure, hormones, girl fights, boys and schoolwork. What may have been an open relationship with Dad can become awkward.

How do you tell your Dad that your period has started and can he please get those sanitary towels with wings and the smallest tampons when she stays with him next? And she needs to straighten her hair and blow it dry with the same hairdryer that she has at Mum.

Dan had not thought of this. He was still busy thinking up plans to visit theme parks and zoos, whilst his eldest daughter was checking out the boys at the Panda enclosure. A bit of background and realisation did wonders.

Dan went on to build on the great relationship he already had with his daughters, realising that whatever reaction *they had, could be interpreted in many different ways. At times he went back to his fear. But most of the time he asked himself the questions that I asked him. He became a confident man-with-balls who was pursuing his happiness in life in all areas.*

A doctor friend shared that he has found almost all healers to be in touch with their feminine energy. The doctors that do not, have a mechanical masculine presence that allows for fixing the physical problem but never connecting with the client. As a healer you must have both. Feminine energy to connect with your patients and clients. And masculine energy to fix the physical problem.

He continues to share that in pursuing his mission in life, he gets very single minded. His partner understands that when he is really focused, it is a bad time to interrupt him. He goes on to say 'I love her dearly, but when I am completely focused and driven, I may even get irritated when asked to focus somewhere else. I believe that this is inherent to masculine energy.'

When I talk about balls, I mean authentic masculinity, not something that you have to force, to invent or conjure up. But it may be that you need to go and find it within yourself as it has been hidden for a while. If you look at different areas of life, you can see that there is a different need for balls in each of the following areas.

Career, physical, emotional, financial, relationships with others, spirituality and environment.

In your career it is important to have balls as this will give you the impetus to move forward or not. Can a person who seems a total beach bum just doing what he wants to do, still have balls? The answer is yes and the words 'just doing what he wants to do' give this away. I know both men and women who do exactly that.

For your physical body, you have various options. Do you choose to exercise and if so, what kind of exercise do you choose? Any exercise can be done from either more masculine or more feminine energy. There are certain sports that make it easier to tap into more masculine energies. Think of individual competitive sports and contact sports. Team sports. Most sports are a healthy outlet for surplus energy and the rules that apply keep players and participants within bounds. Taking responsibility for your physical wellbeing is a sign of being 'grown up with balls'. Do you know what is healthy for you and do you make sure that you have a lifestyle that supports this?

The emotional part of your life is not something to be ignored and suppressed. Neither should it seem that a monster is unleashed. Feeling, witnessing and experiencing your emotions are healthy ways of dealing with this part of your human existence. Again, taking responsibility for feelings and releasing them in a healthy and safe environment is a good choice. Seeking professional help when you feel stuck is not a sign of weakness, but a sign of maturity and insight.

The currency of the world is money. Although we get minimal education during our formal schooling, it does pay to familiarise yourself with the management of finances. Simply because that ensures that the ride of your life feels more smoothly. Ignoring this vital area can lead to times of pain and uncertainty. Whatever your beliefs about money are, it pays (!) to adopt a general notion of abundance and plenty and learn to manage your finances. It is true that even the highest earners without a money management system can end up poorer than an average wage earner with a sound implementation of money management.

In relationships it pays to strap on your balls from time to time. Please do not mistake bully behaviour towards women and children to be masculine behaviour. Many women agree that men being tender and kind from a free and totally masculine place are much more attractive than any showing off in so called 'macho' mode. Speaking to women, one of the sexiest images is the one of a confident man holding a baby.

As the head of the family, you may be the spokes person. You may need to protect your family, your community, members of your extended family or your company. You can support others where needed. You can show loyalty by staying the distance through circumstances that are less than ideal.

Spirituality can be whatever you choose it to be. For some it is a particular religion, for others a strong connection with nature. Yet others want to meditate, dance or sing. As long as this spiritual expression is one of your own choosing? Tapping into your spiritual energy can be a grounding experience, which can calm you down.

Your environment is your responsibility to an extent. Your home, garden, neighbourhood are all co-created by you and with those around you. Make sure to take responsibility for this area too.

Nikolai's Story:

Nikolai was a dashingly handsome man, early fourties, greying temples, penetrating but kind, dark eyes. Perfect olive skin. He had the endearing habit of flicking his thick locks off his forehead with a slight frown. He had women swooning. He was single. A pilot. It seemed that Nikolai had it all. Or, could have it all. He was nice, kind, always doing the right thing. Yet, there was something about Nikolai that gave people the impression of something dark and deep.

No one could put their finger on it. As if there were a secret. During an evening with a friend it all came out. He was in his twenties. A fling. Nothing more. No emotion, no follow up. The girl was pregnant. She had a son. His son. She blackmailed him. For money. Of course. But he could not see his son. She used him. Milked him. For what he was worth. He could still not see his son. He went to court. She won. He had to pay. And he could still not see his son.

Twenty years on. The son is twenty. His twenty first birthday next week. Nikolai is beside himself. Two years ago he was making headway. He got to know Danny. Spent weekends together. Nikolai went out of his way to please the son he never knew. After eight months Danny did not want to see him any more. It wasn't what he wanted after all. He had no time. No real interest. It was nice to get to know his Dad, but there wasn't a place for him in his life.

He called him last week. To plead. Can I see you please? You are my son. You're twenty one. It would mean so much to me. He even cried. Danny stayed silent and then said: 'you're pathetic, what kind of a man are you' and put the phone down.

What to do? Behind the façade of niceness and kindness there was a huge anger with the injustice of it all. Nikolai wanted to please. Was raised to be nice. And kind. Not angry. A nice boy. A nice man.

So many men exist like Nikolai. Angry. Bottled down hurt. And one day that festering creates dis-ease. Nikolai had a bad back. A very bad back. He had to have injections. And it was still bad.

Another man like that flips. And kicks the dog. Or the wife. Or gets a gun. And kills ten people.

Another man like that sighs. Plays computer games. Kills ten people. On the screen. Has a cup of tea. Walks the dog. Goes to bed.

Another man like that looks into his anger. Feels the anger. Feels the pain. Enquires into the violence. Rides the waves of rage. In a safe space. Turns it into energy. Whilst running. Pounding the streets. Sweating like a pig. Or kicking a ball. Or singing solo. Or carving wood. Or building an empire.

What about Nikolai. Could he have done something differently? He was fuelled by guilt. Towards his son.

Exercise:

- What does a career look like when you have balls? Do you have a vision, are you grounded and rooted in what you want?

-Do you take full responsibility for your physical wellbeing? Are you fit? Healthy? What can you do to improve?

-How do you deal with your emotions? Do you have a healthy and safe outlet? Is there anything that you want to change?

-Do you manage your money well? What do you need to learn in order to take control of your financial destiny?

-Are the relationships in your life all healthy? Do you have an intimate relationship? Does it make you happy? How about your partner? How about the relationships with both your parents? Your children? Friends? Family? Is there anything that needs to be put right regarding those relationships?

Note: all relationships are a reflection and gauge as to how well your life in general works.

-Do you regularly connect to a force that is greater than yourself? (You can call this force God, The Universe, The Creator, Mother Nature or anything of your choosing)

-Is your environment of your choosing? If not, what would you like to see changed? (then make a plan to take steps towards that)

Note: Growing up, there are many opportunities for making decisions. About what school to go to, what university, what job to get, what car. And later, what bank to deposit your money with, which holiday to go on. Deciding whether to move out of the parental home or not. Coming out if you're gay. Confronting someone without loosing your temper. Standing up for yourself. Standing up for a cause. Protecting someone.

Which partner to choose? Whether to have a family or not. Changing career. Buying a home. Moving home. The list is endless. You are in charge. All choices bear consequences. Be willing to live with the consequences of your choices.

Finding your own truth

Living your own destiny

Are you here in now?

Chapter Four:

Where are your balls?

That may be an obvious question with an equally obvious answer. Physically we all know where your balls are. Where are they figuratively speaking? Can you say hand on your heart that your balls are where you want them to be?

Sayings such as 'he has no balls', 'she has the balls' and 'you can see who has the balls in that relationship' are all saying something similar: If you are two people who have both consented and are both happy, there is nothing wrong with any of that.

But if you or your partner is not happy, then it is time to look and find out where your balls are and how to get them back.

Here are various scenarios:

Your Balls Are:

In the cupboard: you haven't felt the need for them so have stored them until you may need them at a later date. Question is: are they right there in the first drawer where you have access to them right away? Or do you have to rummage through piles of shoes, bags of socks and ties to find them? Are they dusty and not cherished? Or are they shiny and ready for use?

In the trophy cabinet: they are on display for all to see like all your other trophies. But you are not using them. They are shiny and new from underuse.

The man with the trophy balls will very likely collect other trophies. He has a trophy cabinet with those balls on display and that is a bit lonely. He may want a trophy woman. The trophy woman goes in the trophy cabinet next to the trophy balls. Let's see. Still a bit empty and lonely. Get a trophy car. A trophy house, a trophy pool, a trophy set of golf clubs, shoes, shirts, hat, jacket, the whole caboodle. Before you know it this guy has a jam packed trophy cabinet and just goes through the motions. He is addicted to what his friends have to say 'Gee man, what a great ....(car, wife, set of golf clubs, fill in the blanks). He is not happy though!

Lost: somewhere during your life you felt it was safer to not have them. Maybe you needed to be the 'good boy' and you found that what was stopping you from being the 'good boy' were those darn balls. You deny that you ever had them and can't honestly remember the last time when you did. Life is better without balls (although you are reading this book, so something or someone must have invited you to do so?)

In your partners' purse: it looks that she has emasculated you and it is very peaceful not to make too much of a fuss about it or she will go mental and if you catch her at one of those moods, she may take the rest of your remaining manhood too.

In your mothers' tea cabinet with the rest of her trinkets: oops, you moved out (or maybe you didn't yet?) and Mum still has your balls in custody. You phone her regularly when you need to make important decisions to ask for her advice. If she is on holiday or absent for whatever reason you fret and feel you can't take any decisions until she is back.

Your mother still thinks they are in her tea cabinet, but they really aren't: they are where they need to be, but you forgot to tell Mum. She still phones you to gives you advice on many areas of your life. Most of those areas are none of her business and if anyone else would give you uninvited advice of this ilk you'd tell them where to go. But hey, SHE is your MOTHER! If you have a partner, there comes a point that they do not like this relationship triad.

You swallowed them: not really of course, but you have had to take back your innate and natural power so often that you are blocked in the midriff area of your body. It looks as if the top half of your body seems to be operating separately from the bottom half. You have locked your strength out of your life. Any situation that calls for core strength is another opportunity for you to block this energy. You may even notice a physical blockage in that region.

The boss has them in the safe of the company: you are a loyal worker and the company has replaced the apron strings. You would not do anything without consulting your boss. If you ever get made redundant, you either get depressed forever or may be the guy who throws a noisy big boy tantrum.

In the freezer: they keep well when frozen, but they do get cold. Too cold. You are the proverbial guy who never looses his temper, blows neither hot nor cold. The one the women say has no feelings..... however much they provoke you. Balls on ice.

In the comfy chair: simmering doing nothing. You rather take life easy and if easy is not in the offering, you are not interested. You have found that other people will do things for you as long as you stay in the comfy chair, watching TV, watching the world go by; watching other people do things for you, and watching your life go by without participating in it. So much easier. At the end of your life you wonder where the days have gone and why you haven't done x/y/z.

I am not judging you for any of the above (well, I am really, because I know that there is so much more possible for you if you are prepared to Get Your Balls Back). So that when you take your last breath, you can honestly say that your life was of your choosing.

Henry's story:

Henry was a lovely man. Bright, gentle and caring. He and Mandy had been in an ambling relationship for eight years. Henry developed programs for an educational software company. His days were predictable and up to recently, Henry enjoyed the stability and certainty of the monthly income which was more than generous.

Mandy's career was also in education, in her case more hands on. Mandy was a secondary school teacher. She taught maths to reluctant and hormonal fourteen year olds. Most of them did not enjoy the subject which was a disappointment for Mandy, who loved maths. A passion for her subject had decided her direction in life after University. She had not realised that there could be anyone in the world who did not adore maths!

In her spare time, Mandy was on various boards of very brainy organisations. Henry did jigsaws in the evenings, never sure when Mandy would be back from her self imposed duties. Recently, Henry had increased his hobbies with a spiritual inkling. A neighbour in the street had knocked on his door and invited him to a yurt in his garden for regular meditations. Although Henry had never meditated, he happily obliged and was pleasantly surprised by the gentle, relaxing atmosphere that was created in the yurt. As Mandy was mostly absent, it gave him something to do on lonely evenings.

During his bachelor time, Henry had loved regular outings into complete wilderness. This gave him a thrill and a connection to nature that he really enjoyed. When I met Henry, he told me that he was not sure that Mandy actually was the right life companion for him. Their relationship just kind of happened and he was surprised that they were still there eight years later. Through no fault of his own, Henry was made redundant and started to question everything about his direction in life.

Logically, he arrived at the question whether the relationship needed a spring clean as well. As Henry revisited old passions and dreams, he accidentally stumbled on a website where companions were hooked up with disabled people of various backgrounds. One young man had a lifelong wish to go out into nature, camp out and connect to the Earth. Henry applied instinctively and before he knew it, he was on his way to Norway to hike with young Basil. Basil was ninety percent blind. The pair was part of a larger group of young people with their guides. There was a mildly paralysed girl of about seventeen, a deaf boy with thick glasses and a loud and contagious laugh and about ten more similar teams of enthousiasts. What struck Henry was the passion that each and every person displayed, not only for the trip but for life in general.

Henry learned a lot during this trip. Firstly, how Basil lived life to the full. Secondly, how all of the youngsters approached their disability with humour and a kind of defiance. In the spirit of fun. If any of them could not cross a part of the terrain, all would gather around and as a team, find a way to help the one person across. Some was done on their bottoms, lying down, on the backs of others. Invariably accompanied by cheers and encouragements from the others. It didn't really matter to any of them. Friendships happened instantly and grew until at the end of the trip they were closer than many families would ever be in a lifetime.

On returning, Henry decided to end his relationship with Mandy. At the start of their courting they were in love, but their main values in life were not aligned. To Henry a deep heart connection with nature was part of his passion. To Mandy an academic life with her nose in books and doing research was her first love. It became clear that in order for Henry to allow Mandy her happiness, he needed to let go of what seemed to be security but really was more of a comfort zone and convenience.

There is no growth in comfort. We all have the need to grow.

When the couple released one another, Mandy moved on to meet the love of her life, Terrence, a professor of Physics, whom she met at one of her meetings.

Henry found that one of the other volunteers on the Norway trip had not only become a great friend, but also someone with whom he was able to share his newly found spirituality. On the last night of the trip he found an attractive woman with piled up hair and a summer dress, where before she was just another volunteer with hiking boots, shorts and her hair in a pony tail. It was the easiest of connections, as they had become friends to start with and found the attraction later. Their passion and life together is still a beautiful example of what is possible. In following his vision, Henry stepped into his authentic masculinity, which naturally brought out the feminine in Belle.

Belle and Henry have just had a baby son.

Exercise:

- Where in your life are you putting up with less than you (and your partner?) deserve?

- In your authentic masculine, what action do you need to take?

- What do you need to let go of?

- Who do you need to set free?

Note: often we stay in relationships because we do not want to hurt the other person. In turning this around and asking ourselves the question: do we deny the other person their deserved happiness by hanging on to this relationship? In other words: we hurt the other person more by staying in the relationship than by releasing them.

You may need to ask yourself the question: how will life be if we stay in this relationship another ten, twenty, thirty years? Is this fair on your partner? On you? And if you have them, on your children? What message do you give your children by hanging on to this relationship?

You were born with balls

Decision making powers

Your life's destiny

Chapter Five:

What does it look like to have balls?

The silent man was asked to come on stage. He moved with deliberation. An expression on his face that showed nothing. No excitement. No annoyance. Nothing. He stood on stage. Grounded. No movement. Hands held loosely by his side. A slightly curious and open look on his face. The women giggled. The man looked straight ahead. He seemed to be unfazed.

Another gentleman was asked to join. He danced with gyrating hips. His arms in the air. Big grin on his face. Jeans half way down the forever moving hips. The women in the audience shuffled restlessly. Made unappreciative sounds. Booing was heard. The man looked perplexed. He danced more vigorously. The women booed louder. He seemed confused.

The next guy joined them. He looked around himself sheepishly. He smiled. And pulled his shoulders up by his ears. He glanced in the direction of the audience. No reaction. He seemed relieved.

More men joined these three. Tall ones, short ones, fat ones, skinny ones. White guys, black chaps. Chinese and Italians. Curly haired and bald headed. Scruffy ones, bearded ones and hairless ones. A man in suit and tie. A boy in T-shirt and cut off jeans. Nothing in common. Except that all of them were men.

Women kept making sounds. They were asked to vote with sound. Appreciative sounds and non-appreciative sounds. Those men were brave. Some were annoyed. Some behaved triumphantly but were obviously scared. Had tried to hide. It did not work. They were at a personal development seminar and the topic was attraction between men and women. Most men on the stage were puzzled as what attracts women.

The guy with the gyrating hips was getting (fast!) that his attraction strategy did not work for the majority of the women in the room (some two thousand). The man, who had not moved, still did not move. He seemed the most attractive.

On suggestion of the teacher the gyrator stopped gyrating and the female audience was asked to vote again. The appreciation had gone up. Mmm, he was getting it; he looked to his non-moving colleague and adapted the same stance. More appreciation.

Mr. Gyrator had tried to attract attention to himself. The prancing male bird. The females saw straight through this and dismissed him. Someone who would be absorbed by himself and immersed in his own world. If in relationship with a woman, she would get zero attention from him. All about him.

Ben's story:

Ben left his hometown early. At the age of nineteen he could be seen driving the hippy trail with his Volkswagen campervan. As a good looking young man he attracted girls like a jar of honey manifests bees. Ben would cram the van full with at least five females and drive all across the continent. This would pay for his insatiable hunger to travel as well as provide him with mostly pleasant company. Although he learned early on that between whichever females would inhabit the van, rivalry was commonplace.

He learned how to deal with women in a very natural way. He had put his foot in it a few times and invariable regretted it. He became a master at maneuvering between premenstrual tension, envy and possessiveness which most of the women that he shared the van with, would display at some stage during the six week treks.

Bens' first encounter with Thailand was in the late Sixties. He fell in love with the country and decided to stay. As a young engineer it was not difficult for him to find work in the hotels and resorts that started to become popular around that time. After a few years he felt it was time for him to settle down. He had had the odd relationship back home but was more enamored with the Asian women with their gorgeous features and flashing, white teeth. He found their shyness and innocence charming.

Ben married a local girl, a distant relation of the ruling King. That did not mean that she came with any wealth. I believe her family had to work hard to make ends meet, but as so often in that part of the world, wealth in villages and families was shared between all rather than kept to oneself.

Yanni was a bright young woman with a spark. Enterprising too. She had opened a little shop where she sold produce and handicrafts. This is how Ben met her. He was on the lookout for a gift to send to his mother back home. It would be her Fiftieth and Ben would have liked to be there, but there was no way in the world that he could afford an air ticket at the time. So he roamed the streets and found Yanni's shop.

They got talking. And agreed to a date the following Saturday. He took her to his favourite street restaurant. Wore his best shirt. The one that had not frayed too much. She wore a colourful long skirt with a simple, white blouse. He found that he could see deep in her almost black eyes and fell in love with her.

A year later they married. Another year later she bore their first son, Tom. Tom rapidly had a brother, Sam, and within three years the couple had completed their family with baby Jack. A busy time, but relatives lived close and the couple's new little guesthouse was on the beach, so it was a relatively carefree time too. The boys grew up playing in and around the sea and attending the village school. The family was content and self sufficient.

When Tom reached the age of eleven, Ben realised that education in the little village was limited and really wanted to provide his sons with ample opportunities for their future. The guest house was sold. Air tickets bought. Grandmother who by now was in her sixties roped in to look for rented accommodation. The family arrived early in September. The boys had to go to school just a week later. A big adjustment. Sam and Jack were still in primary school. Tom attended the local secondary school just a five miles bus ride in the next town. Their education took place. The boys adapted reasonably well. Their mother less so. Still, the couple imported Thai spices and ingredients and started a local Thai restaurant. It was successful.

Ten years went by. When Jack finished his exams, the family decided that it was time to move back to warmer climes. With savings and proceeds from the restaurant, they were able to buy a small hotel in a village not far from where they used to live. Tom did not deal very well with the move back. He still commutes back and forth between the two places that he calls his home. Not really sure where he belongs. Ben worries about Tom at times. Sam married a Thai girl four years ago. They have two young sons of one and two years old. Jack has only just got married with a girl who is part Thai and part American. She is stunning. The couple is very happy.

Ben came to see me as he was troubled. Still very happy with his own company, he built a boat. Yanni is reluctant to join him on his trips. She gets sea sick. She spends most of her time with Sam and his family looking after the grandchildren. That makes her most happy. She feels that she is needed and useful. Ben feels that Sam is well under the thumb of his wife, Yundi. Yundi has an air of arrogance. She wants Sam to put pressure on his father.

The wealth that Ben and Yanni have gathered will eventually go to their three sons. Even when this is divided it will still be a substantial sum. Yundi wants the money now. Ben is old is her argument. He doesn't need that money. He lives very frugally. Ben has finally opened the discussion. Well, there wasn't really a discussion. He told his daughter in law how it is. That he is still alive. And that *she has no right to decide what he does with his money.*

Even though Ben is a gentle soul, who does not like to upset people, he felt he needed to speak his truth. He spoke from his authentic masculinity.

From his authentic masculine, as head of the family, Ben knows that looking at the larger picture keeps the relationships healthy.

Simon's story:

Simon has a ladies clothes boutique. He is openly gay. Simon is tall, slim and tanned. He is in his early sixties and has a lot to say about the topic. He has had a life time of observing dynamics of masculine and feminine energies. Below are his views.

In a small market town in the south west, he has made a name for himself. The ladies like him as he does not pose a threat to them. He can be quite outrageously camp and forthcoming with them. Men buy from his shop as his taste is impeccable and he will choose the most exquisite creations for their women.

Simon is happy to be openly gay these days, but it wasn't easy to grow up that way. Homosexuality had only just become legal when he came out and in the small town he grew up, he was regularly beaten up and called a 'pansy' and a 'poof'.

As far as Simon is concerned, mothers play a role in their sons' happiness. When a son has plucked up the courage to share his (possibly long hidden) secret with his parents mothers often play the 'I won't be a grandma' trump card.

His suggestions for young gay men to keep their balls is to be strong, come out and don't fall for any blackmail. He feels that gay boys must leave a small town early or their lives will be made difficult. A bigger town or city allows for different circles of friends and a larger community.

What Simon has noticed in the shop, is that women can't make up their mind. He thinks that goes back to primeval instincts, where women had to create the strongest genes in order for their children to survive. They had to literally 'shop around' and see what was on offer before being able to make up their mind. The same shopping around applies when they come to his shop. They try hundreds of dresses and leave with the one they originally picked.

When a woman comes in the shop with her male partner, she wants his opinion. She asks him 'which one should I take, darling?' and most men who have learned to be nice say 'whichever you want, honey,' thinking they are being kind and generous.

He has seen that more often than not this leaves the woman confused and irritated. It seems that she prefers him to say: 'have that one.' She may want him to be stronger for her. Now, she needs to find her own power and you see a shift in the woman when she does that. It seems to move her away from her femininity.

As far as Simon is concerned, gay men always have had balls, maybe even too much. Some men make him feel more masculine; others make him feel and behave more feminine. In the past, he tried to buy men. That did not work. In the case that they were straight, they'd give it all to their girlfriends. And a straight man will always be straight. Simon has always needed to be needed. That made him feel happier and better. When he was not needed any longer is partners tended to move on.

Simon says that a man is bound to find his balls when he is stripped of everything. When there is nothing left, he has to start again. Like the Jews after the Holocaust. Like the women in liberation. They had nothing, so they got strong and got balls.

56

Exercise:

-Are you true to yourself?

-Is there a situation in your life that you are simply tolerating because you do not want to upset others?

-Is there anything that you need to communicate with anyone? Your partner? Parents? Your children?

-How can you do this elegantly without compromising your own truth?

Dreams you had for long

Go and make your vision real

Live your passion now

Chapter Six:

How to get your balls back

Many men have been raised to be gentlemen. This does not mean that you need to let people walk all over you. Express your needs and stick to your point. If you upset somebody, apologise. When you stop being a 'doormat,' you let your true identity shine out and feel great because you feel authentic. You feel secure in yourself, ready for whatever challenges come your way. You experience more energy and you get where you want to more effortlessly.

Note: when you practice this, be careful not to swing the other way. Becoming a tyrant is not the answer. Really be aware of the effect of your behaviour on others and find a middle ground.

Many women (possibly all?) use 'testing' in a relationship. It is a little like checking whether the batteries in the torch still work. You turn the torch on, you shake it a little, maybe bang it with one hand on the other or even on the table. And then you discover a faint flicker of light. When you bang it a little harder, the light shines brighter.

That in essence is how 'testing' a man goes too. She wants to see if you are unshakable, like the rock she needs in her life. She may ask you questions such as 'how would it be if we sold the beach house and get a penthouse in New York?' or 'what would you say if I cut my hair really short?' or 'I think we should move to Timbuktu'. These questions tend to come when you are deeply engrossed in changing the tyres of your youngest sons bicycle or when you are watching your favourite sports team winning their final match of the season.

Usually it means: I want your attention and I want it now. 'whatever you say dear' is a useful standard answer, but it may not always be appropriate. Before you know it you end up with tickets to Timbuktu or the locks changed on the beach house. An answer such as 'I hear you darling, I am really busy right now, but what you say is very important to me, please ask me that question again in twenty minutes/3 days/two seconds when I can give you my full and uninterrupted attention, as you deserve'.

Of course you must then follow up in the time you said.

Work on your posture. Unconsciously, you may slump, droop your shoulders or sit with a hunched back. Stand tall, chest up, shoulders back, and head upright. Develop a firm handshake (without breaking anyone's fingers).

Walk with a sense of purpose, even if you have no idea where you are going. Stand, sit and move with certainty. Your brain gets more oxygen as you stand more upright and your lungs open more. Your chest will open, and your shoulders broaden.

Did you know that when you slouch and hunch your bottom ribs dig into your abdomen? What happens is that your breathing gets hindered, your stomach and belly stick out and you appear less tall than you really are. With a more upright posture, you notice that you command more respect from both men and women and this in turn will make you feel more certain and visible. People will notice this shift and ask what has happened to you. You have more colour on your face as the oxygen gets inhaled more deeply and gets transported to all areas of the body, versus only the vital organs. If you have a partner, she will feel more safe and protected in your presence.

When you do not embrace your masculine energy, women tend to see you as a 'safe' but uninspiring option. They will seek you out when they need someone to talk to as they would another woman friend.

The outer represents the inner. Both reflect on one another. You can enhance masculine energy with clothing and appearance. Wear simple, neat, unfussy clothes. Stay away from too much detail. Keep jewelry to a minimum. Even though you may enjoy facials and other body grooming, make sure you do not discuss those with your woman or go for more treatments than she does.

Your woman will no longer have to hide her expensive feminine beauty products in case you nick them. It will create a polarity between you that means that your relationship will soar to new and unexpected heights.

If you use grooming products to a great extent, hair gels, many facial products, scents, waxing, manicures and pedicures, eyebrow shaping etc, women may treat you as one of their girlfriends (a safe option but not a hot date).

Stand on your own two feet. You are a grown man. Your mother will always stay special in your life. If you want or have an intimate relationship with a woman, she needs to feel that she is the number one woman in your life. It is not fair to let your partner feel she is constantly competing with your mother for that special place in your heart.

You need to let your mother know that she will always be your mother and she is special and unique in that role. You also need to let her know that you are now in a special relationship and that this relationship takes priority over your relationships with anyone else. It will make your woman feel that you are committed to the relationship and that she does not have to compete for your affection, time, attention and approval. She can start loving your mother instead of having to compete with her. If you don't cut the apron strings you will have the constant battle between your woman and your mother on your hands, and you will feel constantly that you are being made to choose.

Take charge of your destiny, even if you haven't felt like committing to the woman in your life before. Not committing stagnates. Decide whether this woman is right for you. If she is, commit. If not, finish the relationship. So many men are heard to say 'I don't want to hurt or upset her.' What do you think is more upsetting? To be in a relationship with a man who fakes his love for her, or to have the prospect of friendship with a man who can admit that she is just not his soul mate, and he'd rather set her free?

When you commit either way, you get out of this stalemate position. You will notice that other areas of your life move forward when you commit. Evidence from years of energy work has shown me that as soon as you 'unblock' one area, others follow suit.

You may want to take that into consideration when you notice that other areas of your life, such as career, finance and health are not showing as much progress as you expect.

Many men (and women) who have fear of commitment really fear that they will loose their freedom. When asked, they do not really know what kind of freedom they mean. The freedom to do what? If you are used to leave the curtains half open every morning and your partner pulls them all the way open, does that make you feel you have less freedom?

Are you used to put the salt behind the pepper in the kitchen cupboard and now someone comes in and puts the pepper behind the salt? Ask yourself whether it is really that kind of freedom (which sounds more like rigidity and control than freedom) ?

Or could freedom be redefined? The right to be with the person you love and who loves you? Is freedom the choice to spend a large part of your days with someone who puts a huge smile on your face and makes your heart sing? Decide for yourself.

Note: If you do not like committing, you will attract a person who does not commit either. You both give less than 100% to the relationship. It becomes a tit-for-tat situation. If you give me so much love then I will reciprocate with exactly that same amount. If you don't, I will hold back my love too. It becomes conditional. It takes a confident person (with balls!) to keep giving love even when there is nothing coming back your way for some time.

However tough, giving love back at times when there is none coming back, however uncomfortable gives a message of acceptance. You can handle your partner with all her parts, warts and all. If you run at the least tantrum, she gets the message that you can't cope with all of her. And let's face it; all of us are at times unreasonable, upset, angry and sad. Trying to hide our shadows and dark sides causes more harm than being real.

Many of us are scared of commitment because of previous hurt. We try to protect ourselves and may not even want to venture into a relationship ever again. This means that we have to live with that fear forever. We protect our heart against being broken, yet again. But nothing can survive protected. The consequence is that you live your life less than 100%. Fear becomes and stays a dominating emotion.

Ask yourself: 'what is the worst thing that can happen?' Explore the answers you get. The people I work with usually come to the conclusion that if they explore the worst case scenario of everything, they would still survive.

Life gives each of us beautiful, yet at times very painful moments. Growth only happens outside our comfort zone.

George's Story:

He folded his broadsheet newspaper carefully into his lap. His brown, shiny brogues were slightly scuffed but always shined. Mac in the luggage compartment and very unnoticeable briefcase under the seat in front of him. The stewardess brought his drink. Just a sparkling water with a slice of lemon. No ice. That upset his stomach. He boarded the Eurostar in Brussels after the meeting with the translator who was dealing with the European patent office.

Back home, Jane would be waiting with dinner. Surely, after a glass of sherry, or possibly a gin and tonic, she would tell him about her week with the twins. After reading Suzy and Sam their story, Jane and he could sit down to a well deserved shepherd's pie or something else traditional but wholesome.

George knew who he was. He was middle class. He earned

an average salary. He had been with the same company for the last twelve years. He had job security. He met Jane at a dinner party with his parents some ten years ago. They got engaged a year later and married another six months afterwards. The honeymoon was in the Caribbean which although quite extravagant, was very romantic. Neither Jane nor George had ever travelled that far afield before their honeymoon or since.

Their cottage in the country was roomy but cosy. The couch was inherited and re upholstered. The dining suite had been George's Grandmothers and was some hundred years old. It was polished weekly and had been for the last ninety five years. Beeswax. The best. The chairs creaked. Needed some attention.

During the weekends George would spend time in his garage with his beloved Jaguar E-type which he managed to purchase inexpensively through a friend who knew an old chap where the low mileage vehicle had been unused and tucked away in a garage.

On Saturdays Jane took Sam to rugby and Suzy to ballet. They would alternate the Sunday lunch at either Jane's or George's parents.

George dealt with the finances of the family, and Jane brought up the children and made sure that the house looked tidy and clean.

Jane did not work. She was trained as a secretary, but gave this up as soon as she got married to George.

George did not like the idea of his wife working. Jane never questioned this. She seemed to be happy with her plight as was George. Jane was a participant at one of the workshops I ran in that part of the country. She felt there was something missing in her life. George was kind and her life was okay. But a bit dull. Everything was so very predictable. After a few private sessions, Jane remembered her own passions. She really wanted to start a small recruitment agency for secretarial workers. She broached the subject with George. He asked her if she wanted more money? She didn't. Just needed more of a sense of fulfillment in life now that the twins were at school most of the time. She got in touch with a few friends from before her marriage and they brainstormed ideas.

After a few sessions the idea of a business was born. George was consulted as were other partners and husbands. A business plan made, a loan from the bank secured. George got used to the idea and supported Jane's business whole heartedly when he saw how Jane blossomed and grew into the woman he admired and loved before.

George acts from his authentic masculine. Although he initially does not like the idea of his wife working, in witnessing her growth and sense of satisfaction, he abandons these ideas.

Jim's story:

He was dancing, shimmying hips, hands touching himself. Sliding over his body. He did not look around him. He was engrossed. In himself. The moves got larger. In complete rhythm with the music. His carefully built quiff, quivered as the music swept faster. His frenzy was complete. Only then did he look around him. Who had seen him? The girl in the corner eyed him. She was drinking a green drink from a tall glass with a long straw. Looking down in the glass he noticed that she went cross eyed.

He smiled. Back to his dance. His number three shaved chest glistened with sweat. Manicured hands, pedicured, smooth feet. The few hairs that unsighted his back were waxed off this morning by Max, ouch the thought made him wince.

The metro sexual man was born not that long ago. There is largely no need for a man to look and behave like a man in the old fashioned way. So why not pinch some of what women have owned for centuries? Why not preen, cultivate, manicure and pedicure? Straighten, wax, gel and veneer? Implant, suction, extend and grow? Pluck, clip, moisten and remove? Leisure time extends and work time lessens. Contraptions make life less demanding. Dirty hands a thing of the past. It makes sense to manicure. It looks tidy to wax. It is in line with fashion to straighten and pluck.

Fly away hair a thing of the past with the right conditioner. No excuses for nose hair, or ear hair. There is an implement for trimming those. Unsightly toe nails? Pedicure! Unruly chest hair? Electric razor set to a perfect number three! Over flowing Speedo's? Brazillian! Trends dictate that we need to look a certain way. And of course manufacturers jump on the bandwagon with advertising as they have dollar signs in their eyes.

Exercise:

-How do you want to present yourself?

-Look through this chapter and decide what you want to take on regarding to posture, clothes and behaviour.

The words that make you

Building blocks of you are

Speak your truth in words

Chapter Seven:

What do you say?

Masculine language is precise, to the point and uses words that express going forward and taking charge. Words of support, of loyalty and protection. These will make you feel more certain, confident, and able to deal with the world at large. When you talk in this manner, people know that you mean business. That you are strong and capable. Even if you don't feel this way to start with, with practice this becomes a habit. Before you know it, it is even automatic.

Use language that make you feel more certain and self assured. Language that indicates vision and moving forward. Not a string of abuse or swear words. That shows immaturity and insecurity but can be used occasionally to emphasise a point.

The words we use determine the way we feel. If we want to change the way we feel, we must change the words we use.

Adam's Story:

Adam had moved to the Far East to start a new life. A life change for him and his wife Marianna. They left Poland a decade ago and the life they envisioned in England did not quite turn out the way they expected. With debt but good prospects they said farewell to the cold country in February.

As Adam and Marianna were very organised, their move caused minimal upheaval. They had not reckoned with the emotional effects of being even further away from their Polish family and starting (yet again) over in a new country.

Although the couple had a healthy relationship, there were signs of tension. The optimistic view that Adam had taken was based on research done in the US and the

UK. The Asian market was alien and hard to crack for an outsider. When Adam came to me, he was upset that he could not make the money he said he was going to and despondency had set in. This manifested by his not getting up before nine in the morning and not starting work much before lunch time. His reasoning was that he worked many evenings so staying in bed was very tempting.

His energy was low and he did not sound very passionate about his health business. To be true, he sounded tired and a bit fed up. He used words such as 'I guess' and 'I will try,' 'the people here seem less motivated,' 'I am not sure that I am in the right place' and 'maybe it will work.' He asked for help with his energy and his motivation. Every time he found a potential prospect he needed time to tell them of the benefits of his products. He felt he could not have this initial session within at least a week. He seemed to lose a lot of productive time and momentum.

A colleague who turned prospects around in less than twenty four hours made Adam think that he could do the same and build his business faster.

He examined his language. He agreed that the words he used were not very convincing. The first thing he did was change these words. He committed to using phrases such as 'I will' and 'I know that I am in the right place.'

After a week, Adam felt more energy. Over time he committed to getting up earlier. He now gets up at six thirty in the morning, which means that he has an extra two and a half hours added to his work day. Those first few hours have become his most productive time of the day. He gets things done that he would have left before. He now speaks to every prospect within twenty four hours and his business has gone up and is starting to thrive.

The relationship has improved too. Marianna confessed that because she was fearful of the failing of the business, she started to doubt Adam. She admitted that his use of words did not reassure her in the slightest.

More Masculine Words and Phrases:

Must

Never

Focus

Know

Prove

No

Do

Now

Action

Done

Which

I never go back on my word

I'll think about it

I never go back on my word

Great!

That is interesting

I like it

We have a good relationship

We keep each other on our toes

That's nice

Let's eat

I'll phone the garage to get the car fixed

Let me take some money out of the cash point

I have sorted things out with the headmaster

The solution to this is...

I have ordered a new sofa

I've booked a table for 8pm.

Come on, let's go.

Eric's Story

I met Eric during a workshop. A broad, smiling, tall giant of a man. Wavy, thick blond hair, regular teeth and chiselled features. Slightly overweight. He seemed a little lost and was wandering around when I bumped into him during a break in a workshop. He shared with me that he was from Finland. He had that quiet, grounded quality about him that I notice often in people who spend a lot of time in solitude in nature. Sure enough he had spent his childhood almost in isolation, in a house in the woods, far away from anywhere.

He went to University in Helsinki, the capital. He had to get used to the crowds of people and general busyness of the place. During his last year there, he met Mette, a Danish girl. He showed me a picture. A gorgeous, vibrant, healthy and happy looking lady. Mette and Eric started a successful seminar business in Helsinki and were making quite a name for themselves. A sad smile appeared on Eric's face. I looked at his body language. He was tall, but he was slumped and his shoulders were hunched and down. His breathing was quite shallow.

Mette had put him on the spot. Although his university degree in marketing and psychology was going to be of little use, Eric was drawn to go back to the family business. His ailing father had hinted that his only son would be of great use right now. Mette wanted to stay in Helsinki or even go back to Denmark to expand the business. I could see that this kind giant was torn. He wanted to please the love of his life and at the same time, he could not let his family down.

I asked him why it was important for him to comply with his father's wish. He told me that there was nothing else he could do, as he was expected to continue the business. He was afraid that Mette would end the relationship and he was sure that he wanted her by his side for life. The two scenarios just did not seem to go together. In all this, Eric did not know which way to move. He felt that he would fail one or the other. So he did nothing. He had even begun overeating, he confessed, just to get away from all the feelings.

I asked him who he was. He was confused. 'Eric, of course' he replied, a bit annoyed. 'I mean deep down inside, who are you?' 'What kind of person?' He was starting to think. 'You can close your eyes if that makes it easier' I said. His breathing got deeper as he searched inside. 'I am a strong man, a powerful man,' he said hesitantly. Then he went back to his fears 'But I see no way out, it is driving me crazy.' His breathing went shallow again, shoulders slumped again. I could see this man's pain.

'You come from a people who are fearless and have to make decisions instantly, Eric, who were they?' I asked. 'Warriors, people who lived through adversity, hardship and had to cope with the most strenuous condition in weather, they are some of the toughest people I know. When I grew up these people were my heroes,' he spoke softly.

He stood up straighter now, breathing deeper. 'What part of them is in you, Eric?' I asked. He stood even straighter, head up, smile around his lips 'Well, really....., all of them is part of me' he said. 'What would you call that part?' I asked. 'The Viking' he replied. 'Ok, Eric the Viking....mmm, what would he do in a situation like this?' A smile appeared on his face. He stood strong now, with renewed energy. His legs firm, planted and unmoving.

'I would find a solution to have both, to be with my woman and to continue both my family business as well as my seminar business.' He was getting excited now. He could see possibilities. 'And would Eric the Viking overeat to avoid these decisions?' was my next question. 'Absolutely not. Eric the Viking needs to be healthy so that he can guard his energies to be able to do all he needs to do in this lifetime. Which is a lot. And he will.' A different man opened his eyes, gave me a bear hug and went on to live his life.

Every once in a while I get a message from Eric the Viking. About how the family business thrives, how proud he is to be a Dad, for the first and second time. And how Mette and he run their seminar business in the whole of Scandinavia. How Mette has blossomed into the true, strong feminine woman that she is now allowed to be. How he enjoys the challenges that come his way. How he loves solving the problems that life gifts him with.

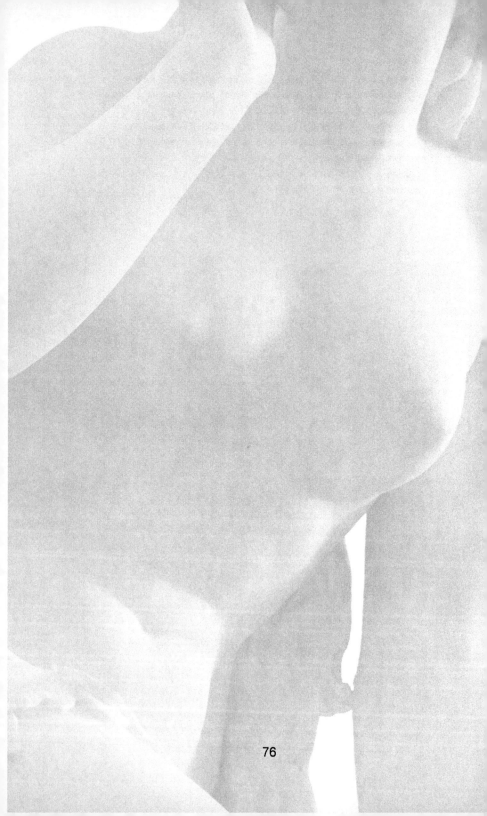

Exercise:

-Which three words or phrases do you use consistently that make you feel insecure or doubt yourself?

-Which three alternatives can you choose that make you feel confident?

-Do you have conflicting situations in your career life?

-What do you need to remember about yourself and the generations that have come before you in order to make those situations move forward and work for you?

Note: today's society does little to remember our ancestors. You may find that some of them have actually dealt with situations that resemble yours at the moment. I have found it worthwhile to look back through the family line and meditate on these long passed family members. My own family travelled over continents in times when this was highly unusual. All the females were entrepreneurial adventurers. I was able to tap into resources that lay inside me, dormant, passed on through DNA and accessible.

Mothers, girlfriends, wives

All are keepers of your balls

Go and get them back

Chapter Eight:

A Chapter for Women

I am aware of my tendency to arrange, organize, plan and oversee most areas of life. I am a strong woman. Independent. This attitude is very useful when I lead my business, conduct workshops, consultations, and seminars and travel the world.

As a girl growing up, my Mum used to say 'make sure you never end up depending on a man.' Because of feminism and woman's liberation I and many women in the West are in this privileged situation. I feel enormous gratitude to the sisterhood that has gone before me to ensure women have the right to vote, to work, to have equal opportunities in the workplace, to have ample childcare to return to our careers. I feel indebted to those women pioneers that have literally risked their lives to guarantee women of today the freedom that many of us have now and take for granted.

After 'Give Him Back His Balls' was published, some women felt that I advocated going back to the days before feminism. That I wanted them to go back to the 'kitchen sink.' This is not what I want for you. If you choose to, please do go wherever you want to. Including the kitchen sink.

A famous Dutch actress (Belinda Meuldijk, who wrote the Foreword for the Dutch version of 'Give Him Back His Balls') sums the message up in one word (thanks Belinda).

> *"What Brigitte Sumner wants for women is 'E-woman-cipation' versus 'e-man-cipation'. Not to become a man in our striving to be equal, but to keep our identity as women and draw on the power that being a woman gives us. "*

What I want for women as well as men is to share the beauty, love and spiritual growth that an intimate relationship can bring.

'I am an independent woman' can give the message 'don't approach; I don't need anyone in my life. If you do enter my life, you will be redundant and will have no value to add.'

I found that the tendency to arrange, organise and control all was not working in my relationship with Rex. It created competitiveness. There was less polarity and more of a 'roommate' feeling between us. In 'Give Him Back His Balls' I go more into detail about the dynamics. Please feel free to read a free chapter on my website www.brigittesumner.com. Stepping out of the masculine energy in my relationship with my husband Rex, vacated the space energetically for him to step into that energy, which in turn enabled me to act more from my authentic feminine energy.

What I found more and more in working with others in my coaching business is the following: there is so much more to explore in relationship when we, women, are prepared to become vulnerable, open up, give up control. There is so much more available if we allow our men to step into their core masculine energy.

It is up to us, mothers, women, girlfriends and wives to acknowledge that there is another side than the feminine to our sons, husbands, boyfriends, fathers and friends. Being aware and accepting of that masculine energy is a true gift for us and anyone male in your life.

There has been research lately that shows that the 'feminisation of our schools' is not serving boys (Jill Parkin, Deborah Orr)

Jamie's Story:

It was his first week at school. Jamie had found it so hard to settle in. Home was a farm. He grew up in nature. The lambs were his friends. Hide and seek was a game done with the free range hens in pursuit of their eggs which they managed to lay in different places daily. His pony would take him faster than his own little legs could carry him. At bedtime, Jamie would be tired from running and exciting adventures. From cooking with Mum and mending fences with Dad.

Sitting still was new. And not easy. Jamie was constantly distracted by new stimuli. A colourful doll in the make belief house in the corner. A jigsaw with bright coloured balloons. Tracy's pigtails with irresistible bows to pull (he'd done it twice now, the teacher had scolded him).

Playing was done quietly at school. Whispering was good. Shouting was bad. Yelling was bad too. Sitting down good. Running around not good. Jamie was learning. But it was so tiring. His whole young life he had been on the go. It was all good. The only time he had done different was when visiting Aunt Ella in town. Aunt Ella lived in an apartment. With small rooms. Like boxes. And no garden. But she did have a balcony. With flower pots. And a television. That Jamie had watched all the while that Mum and he had been there. As there was nothing else to do.

Jamie is one of the little boys that come to education and finds that there are many things that feel unnatural to him. Sitting still. Being quiet. Only speaking when you are asked. Going to the toilet when you have been given permission. Schools as we know them started as an initiative in the Prussian army. From an early age, we reward feminine behaviour in our boys. We want 'good boys.'

I don't think that there is anything gained by boys and men having to feel 'wrong' for being and feeling masculine. How can we serve both our boys and girls in their upbringing? How can we create more of a 'boy friendly' environment, where we don't constantly give them the message that being a boy is being wrong?

Jenny's story:

Jenny always seemed to be the life and soul of the party. She was bubbly, vivacious and strong. A loud and sunny laugh would always announce that Jenny was in the house. Rick, her boyfriend was a soft spoken guy. He would not speak more than needed. He was always there for Jenny.

Jenny was divorced. She had two children, a little boy of

81

nine and her daughter was eleven. Jenny said she had to be strong for both of them during the messy divorce which had taken the best part of a year. She ensured that both children did not get behind with their schoolwork and made a point that even during the tough financial times, the children did not lack in anything.

When I met Jenny, she wanted to hide under the bed covers. It was as if her world had collapsed. She confided in me that she was really a shy person. It took all her energy to pretend that she was confident. That she did not really like to be in the lime light. That the whole last year had taken its toll on her health. She had developed Irritable Bowel Syndrome and was on anti depressants.

Rick had recently remarked that he did not feel their relationship was going anywhere. Jenny was at the end of her wits. She broke down one morning and felt really awful.

She hated feeling like this. She did not want to lose Rick. But she did not know how to go on. There was just so much to do. It seemed that everyone relied on her to arrange and organize everything. She was clearly overwhelmed and scared.

Jenny started to express her fears. What would happen if she let go of all the things she had done up to now? The children might not revise. The house could get messy. The ironing would not be done. She would feel out of control. And she did not like that idea. She preferred things to be the way she wanted them and not really any other way.

She was tired though, exhausted really. Could Rick do more in the house they had recently bought together? If she let him, would it be ok if the towels were folded in three rather than four? Would it be ok if her daughter did some cooking and made a mess? How about her son clearing up his room and even sweeping his own tiled floor?

Jenny's first week was tough. There was dust under her

son's bed. Her daughter burned the scrambled eggs. Nick folded the towels differently and there was no ironing done. Yet, Jenny went to a few fitness classes; she finally walked the dog and went to the sauna. She did feel great.

She tried on her true persona. The shy one. The one that would listen and allow others to do things. For her. She learned that Rick was actually a very supportive man. If she let him. Which she did. Over time.

Over time, Jenny remembered more of her feminine core. Organised less. Let things happen more naturally. It felt scary to start with. She had less control this meant that things happened. Not 100% the way she had envisioned them. But they did happen nonetheless.

The children did more. Rick was there for her. Now that she let them. She told me that Rick had changed. Was more decisive. Arranged more. Took more initiative. Organised more. Did more. The couple were in a good space. Happy to support one another in a balanced and healthy way.

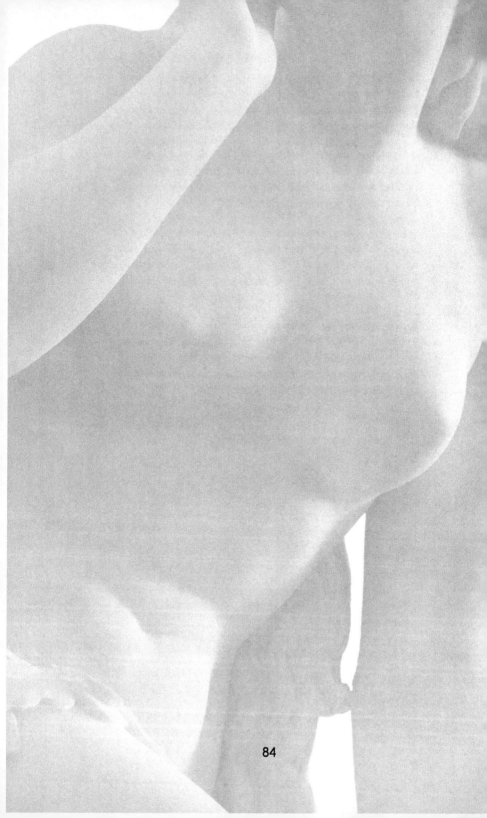

Exercise:

-Do you need to allow someone in your life space to step into his masculine energy?

-What could you do to give them that space? Do you need to trust? To let go?

Note: Make sure to get together with your girlfriends, read a book that you wanted to for ages or have an early night. Let your man have his nights out with his mates.

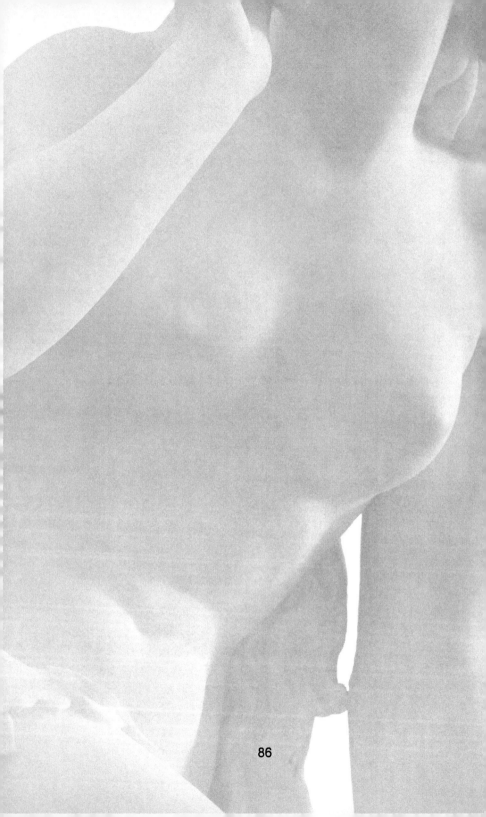

Mark's story

Mark was a successful global manager for an Ice cream supplier. A dashing and dynamic young man, he was quick witted and intelligent and was proud to have climbed the corporate ladder relatively quickly. He travelled at least two weeks per month to far away places, stayed in five star hotels and was frequently asked to attend glamorous functions to do with his job. His new wife Amy was proud of her husband to start with. She did not work herself but did a lot of volunteer and charity work which would keep her busy in the local community. A good spokes woman and lovely looking, she was never without company.

As time went on, Amy started to miss Mark. Just as they settled into their life together, Mark had to hop on a plane again. They had a few arguments and Amy finally begged Mark to find work locally. This pained Mark, who as well as being besotted with the gorgeous Amy, was passionate about his job and proud of what he had achieved.

Finally Mark could bear it no longer, it was the fifth time that his wife had stood in the airport, whaling and clinging on to his sleeves as he was about to take off. His heart was torn. This had to stop. He handed in his notice secretly. His colleagues told him he was mad. Mark knew he did this to save his marriage. When he returned from his next trip to the Far East he told Amy that he had a huge surprise for her.

Not long after, Mark bought a small cottage in the country where they would run the local village shop to create an income. It took a while to adjust as Mark was so used to the five star life style and travel. It was a bit of a sacrifice. Mark did not mind. He adjusted to village life beautifully. What happened with Amy was a different story though. She was not happy. She found that having her husband around all day every day was actually a big disappointment.

She missed her freedom. She missed the attention from other men. No more duty free perfumes, no exotic gifts from far away places. It took her a while to adjust to small village life. In fact, she didn't. The supposed love nest became a bit of a hornets nest with the couple arguing frequently.

The village shop was less of a romantic reality than the imagined dream. The couple had to work long hours. Amy's beautifully painted nails got chipped. Her hair was unkempt. Mark would frequently work in just jeans and a T-shirt. No more handsome, handmade suits, pressed with razor sharp seams. The couple would look at each other and wonder where the gorgeous and handsome partner had gone.

Mark's ex-colleague John came to visit in his new Porsche convertible. Just back from a trip to Hong Kong and Sri Lanka, John was lean, tanned and enviable in Marks' eyes. He was everything she had lost in her husband and desirable in Amy's eyes. There was an obvious spark. Before long, Amy moved out of the love nest and into John's arms. She has picked up her previous lifestyle of charity work again. She does not complain about John's absence. Her nails are perfect as is her hair.

Mark could not believe what happened to him. His jaw still drops when he regales people with the story. After the initial bewilderment he is resentful. But Mark takes life as it comes. He still has the pictures to show his great lifestyle. He has restored the village shop with love and affection. It is not his dream, but he now takes great pleasure in providing local entertainment by semi insulting his customers, who love him. He has taken up painting and horse riding. He is a man of many talents.

Exercise:

-Men: Have you been or are you in a relationship where your partner is not happy with your career? If so, is your career of your choosing?

-Would you be willing to review your current career path and change it?

-Are you aware that this could lead to your partner still being unhappy?

-Women: Have you tried to persuade a partner to give up his passion?

-Are you aware that this could lead to you still being unhappy?

-Is there another solution to reaching your happiness?

Note: The inauthentic feminine, which we can all display, tests to find out how steady the masculine energy is, how much like a rock. Is he easily swayed? Can he stand by his word like a rock? Or does he waver when he is pushed or pulled about?

90

Julian's Story:

Julian is a fourty something, spectacled man of average height. He usually wears chino trousers and an open shirt. His job in security calls for uniforms during his days, so when he gets home, he enjoys the freedom of casual clothes.

Julian is a bachelor. He has had some relationships, but recently decided that he prefers to stay alone. Relationships are too much hassle and Julian is pretty happy on his own. He plays golf with a group of other single men during the weekends and enjoys foreign travel. He likes the freedom that his single status affords him.

Growing up, Julian was the middle boy between an older sister and a younger brother. His sister Sally lives with her husband and their three teenage children not far from Julian in the same region. At times, Julian visits, but he is pleased that he does not have to deal with teenagers himself. From what he can see, Sally and her husband really let their kids rule the roost. As they have chosen to educate their children privately, their lifestyle seems to be compensated by the lack of finances. And it looks as if it hasn't been a worthwhile investment as the youngest is dyslexic and struggles with his schoolwork and the eldest is dabbling with drugs.

Julian's younger brother, Neil is a publisher of an upmarket leisure magazine. Julian is never sure whether Neil is in a relationship or not. Neil does not talk about it. All three siblings are still close to their mother, Susan. Even closer since their father died two years ago.

Susan has recently moved to a bungalow to be closer to both Julian and Sally. Her hip replacement eighteen months ago also meant that stairs were out of the question. Although Susan is very independent, she does rely on her children for quite a lot. Especially Julian has been very helpful. And this was reciprocated by Susan, who always opened her heart and door when Julian needed a listening ear after his

91

relationships went sour.

As Susan and her husband never had any arguments during their long time together, she would shake her head whenever her son rang her to report yet another heated discussion with a partner. She did not understand why anyone should have arguments. She had finally advised Julian that he should not put up with anyone who argued.

Every Sunday Julian went home to have lunch with his mother. This was welcomed by Susan who admitted to be a bit lonely after Bill passed away. Mother and son are very close.

In fact when I meet Julian, he has just come off the phone with Susan, whom he will visit after our session. It is his relationship with his mother that he wants to talk about. He met a woman. Just recently. They started to date. But it was becoming difficult as his mother expected him to be around most evenings and weekends.

And if he wasn't, she would sulk. And he did not want to upset her. After all, it was only two years since Bill died. Julian would like to see his lady friend more often and explore the possibility of a relationship. Julian had a conversation with his mother. Told her how much he appreciated, loved and treasured her. That he would always be there for her. And that he met a lady with whom he had started a relationship. Susan was happy for her son. She has her son's best interest in mind.

Exercise:

-Women: Do you feel that a man in your life should not pursue his vision? Would that interfere with their growth and happiness?

-Men: Do you feel that a woman in your life is stopping you from what you want to do? If so, could that be because she is afraid? What do you need to address in your next conversation with her?

-Are you willing to tell the truth as it is in order for you and her to grow? What do you need to let go of?

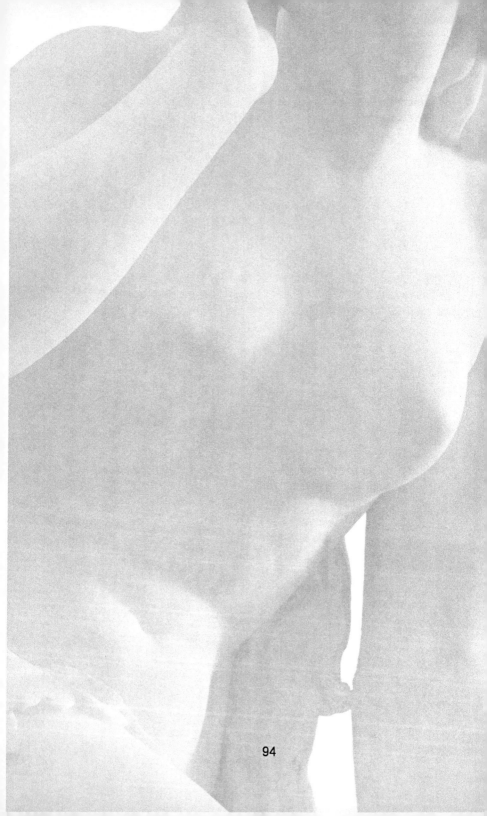

Epilogue

This book is an invitation. To explore. I have seen and witnessed so much pain in relationships. Most people say they would like to be in one. Only to be disappointed. Hurt. And suffer from heartbreak.

So often we flee into a relationship in order to escape from certain conditions and circumstances. I encourage you to explore the possibility that setting your relationships in life right, sets your life right and is your path to happiness. Isn't life just that? A whole journey of relationships?

Wishing you all happy relationships and peace in your soul.

Acknowledgements

With my deepest gratitude to the men of my family: Papa, my brothers Ed and Eric, Opa van Rooijen, Ton, Jan, Menno, Jos, Ger, Michel, Louis, Lucien, Armand, Frank, Robbert-Jan, Erik, Arjen, Opa Liat, Wen Bin, Xiao Bin, Duan Lang, Tjong Ho, Djie Thay Hien, Tony, Sharif, Michael and many others.

My friends Hal, Rod, Darren, Chris, Karl, Don, Gary, Dave, Sean, Marlong, Gary, Felix, Shore, Scott, Michael, Gef, David, Stuart, Alexander, Andrew, Lex, Gerry, Tad, Ted, Kieron, James, Pa, Peter, Chuck, Victor, Bill, Brian, George, Gordon, and all you men out there who have been brave enough to share your stories, to be examples and to open your hearts. Thank you.

The young men who continue to inspire me: Matt, Enrique, Pat, Hugo, Ashley, James, Steven, Dario, Nikolai and all young men I have met over the years at GYLS. You own the future.

Deep gratitude and a sense of belonging to all the women in my family: Mam, Oma Jojo, Oma Mien, my 'bonus mum' Caro, Jose, Meihua, Yu Xin, Git, Rudi, Marian, Christine, Marlies, Xandra, Jolanda, Bernadette, Marian, Marjan, Linda, Irma, Jong, Chen Chu, Bertha, Rita, my mother in law Tasha, my nearly Mum Cees and Mother of the heart Tina.

To my girl friends and sisterhood: Doris, Brenda (your coaching helped me to nail it), Patty, Connie and Deborah. To Amanda Jane (your years of coaching finally got some results, I am a slow learner!),Phillippa, Marianne (you are always in my heart and are like a sister), Dipti, Lizzi, Linda, Geeta, Janice, Heidi, Vicki, Buzz, Vicki, Loren, Kathy, Pam, Mary, Marie, Jette, Amanita, Becky, Debra, Mimi, Tammy, Sumadi, Yanni, Ronny, Sherry, Kim, Felicity and Susie and the many of you who have touched my heart and shared your journeys with me.

To the many teachers that shared their wisdom with me: Yap Cheng Hai, Gordon Merfield, Yap Leong, Samadarshini, Karel Gietelink, Wouter de Kruiff, Krishna Raj, Theo de Wit, Hans Stam, Tom Matena, Ananda Giri, Eva Libgott, Andre Wahlen, Dr. Koos Slob,

Ad van Hasselt, Brian Mayne, Joep de Graaf, Choa Kok Sui, Mikao Usui, Tony and Sage Robbins, Allan & Barbara Pease, John Gray and Deepak Chopra.

Thank you to Margot, Andrew, Ray and Marie, Kari, Billie, Vicki, Joe, Joseph, Isobel, Foxx, Mac, Harry, Karl, Peta, Jette and Belinda.

All of you continue to inspire me.

My deep thanks to the two young men that I am blessed to witness growing up, my sons Jez and Lionel.

And finally, my husband, soul mate and best friend Rex, I thank you and I love you so very much.

Resources:

Anand, Margot – *The Art of Sexual Ecstasy* Harper Collins

Brizendine, Louann M.D - *The Female Brain* Random House. *The Male Brain* to be published in 2010

Campbell, John - *The secret of intimate relationships* Wise Owl Secrets

Deida, David - *The Way of the Superior Man* Sounds True, Inc.

Firebrace, Peter and Sandra Hill - *A guide to Acupuncture* Constable

Geary, D. C - *Male, female: The evolution of human sex differences.* American Psychological Association.

Gray, John – *Men are from Mars, Women are from Venus* Harper Collins

Hill, Napoleon - *Think and Grow Rich* Carpstone

Kimura, Doreen - *Sex Differences in the Brain; The Hidden Mind* Special Editions

MacCoby, Eleanor - *The Two Sexes-Growing up apart, coming together* Harvard University Press, 1998

Pease, Allan and Barbara —*Why Men Don't Listen and Women can't read Maps* Broadway

Phillips, Melanie - *The Sex-Change Society: Feminised Britain and the neutered male* The Social Market Foundation

Sumner, Brigitte - *Give him Back his Balls* My Voice

Tannen, Deborah - *You just don't understand: Women and Men in Conversation* Virago Press

My website:

www.brigittesumner.com

I run regular events, workshops and retreats,

Have a look at the events calendar on the website.

Please feel free to share your experiences and feedback with me:

Brigitte@brigittesumner.com

Lightning Source UK Ltd.
Milton Keynes UK
07 September 2010

159577UK00001B/2/P